Growing Pains

From Hurting to Healing

Written By: Sandra Loyd

Copyright © 2023

All Rights Reserved

Publisher: The Mason Publishing Company

This Book contains privacy of the author you cannot copy or duplicate this book all rights reserved. No part of this publication may be reproduced, stored in a retrieval system, or transmitted in any form or by any means -electronic, mechanical, photocopy, recording, or any other- except for brief quotations in printed reviews, without the prior permission of the publisher. For information address:

Themasonpublishingcompany@gmail.com

printed in the United States of America

ISBN: 979-8-218-95355-3

Table of Contents

Title Page

Copyright Page..1

Table Of Contents..2

Acknowledgements..3

Dedication...5

Introduction..6

Chapter 1 Watts...8

Chapter 2 Childhood...17

Chapter 3 Independence..27

Chapter 4 My mother's keeper....................................33

Chapter 5 Love at first sight..40

Chapter 6 Taking a leap of Faith................................48

Chapter 7 Heading into the unknown.......................52

Chapter 8 The Aftermath...61

Chapter 9 Self-Care..75

Chapter 10 Listening to my intuition.........................82

Acknowledgments

I give gratitude to God for restoring my Trust and Faith in him during times when I felt lost and alone. Many blessings to my parents Terri Sims and Sidney Phillips for everything you have instilled in me because I wouldn't be who I am today without you. Love to my children Dartonyon Jr and Darryn for motivating me and showing me what true unconditional love is. Deep appreciation to Nakendra Harris-Mason for encouraging and believing in me during discouraging times. Last but not least, Thank You to all my family and friends who've shown their true support and kept me in their prayers throughout my life. Without your help, I wouldn't have been able to help others.

Dedication

I would like to dedicate this book to my late husband Dartonyon Loyd. I'm so grateful that God had granted me the opportunity to have experienced such a beautiful union with a loving and devoted husband. I will always cherish and never forget the beautiful memories that we've created.

Introduction

While struggling to get adjusted to my new normal after the death of my husband, I found myself feeling lost and unfulfilled in life. This desperate need of wanting to express built up emotions gave me an idea to enroll in a creative writing class. I went into this class not knowing what to expect, where to start, or even what to write, but what I did know was that some of the craziness that I've experienced in my life was worth sharing with the world. I'm a private person so I was indecisive about publishing this book and being in the spotlight, but I knew if I shared my stories, I could possibly help someone who has been through or is currently going through the same situations that I have. Choosing to communicate my thoughts, fears, emotions, and desires on paper has been extremely therapeutic for me and hopefully you'll find it to be a positive coping mechanism for you too.

Chapter 1

Watts

When I tell people I'm from the city Watts, they automatically associate it with ghetto, negative stereotypes, an impoverished neighborhood filled with gang wars, and people who are from Watts are automatically deemed as inferior to some folks.

Growing up in Watts, I felt an indescribable sense of community because the majority of everyone knew each other. Most of us wanted to help each other in some sense. Believe it or not I grew up with a group of great friends and a family that did their best to shield me from a lot of the nonsense going on around me. We've all experienced various levels of hardships that would usually break a person down physically and mentally, but those troubled experiences are in fact what made us stronger. Struggling and dealing with the lack of economic resources really motivated us to strive for better in every aspect of life. There was this deep knowing that we could only try to level up from the environment we were living in.

My life wasn't perfect, but I could look around and see it could have been a lot worse. Growing up in Watts helped me become the woman I am today by building my character and adapting to challenging situations I had to deal with personally. No, I did not live the street life but growing up in an environment around constant drug use, gang violence and poverty has definitely had an impact on me, my family, and the decisions that I make in my life today. My grandparents moved during the Great Migration from the South to California to escape oppressive laws for better living conditions and of course work opportunities. Coincidentally, my mom and dad grew up living right next door to each other and became high school sweethearts. They got pregnant at a very early age and decided to move in together. I have one older brother and two step siblings.

In the 80s, there was a huge crack epidemic that my family was not exempt from. All my life I have known my mom to abuse drugs and alcohol and that was the exact reason why she gave birth to me prematurely. I had to stay in the hospital for months and when I did come home, I had to wear a heart monitor. My mom's addictions caused my family to separate because my dad felt defeated and could no longer help her. My dad did everything he could to keep us together, so it crushed him to make the decision to go his separate way. Even though my dad decided to live his life separately, I still remember when he would come to our apartment to check on us after work. I remember always being so excited to see him because in my eyes he was like Santa Clause, he would always bring us food, fill our pockets with money, and spoil us with brand new clothes and shoes. My dad is the type of guy that likes to look at the lighter side of things in life with humor. He would always tell me this story about when my mom would use me as a pawn when she would get mad at him when he did try to visit. She would have me lock the screen door on him and tell him to go back to where he came from. He said, then I would have to bribe your little fat ass with Nestle crunch bars and pizza to make you unlock the door. I'm telling y'all my dad is funnier than Eddie Murphy. Well at least to me he is. He's one of the people I call on when I'm feeling down, and I want to take my mind off things with a good laugh.

Despite my mom's addictions, she had a sweet side to her too and that is what I love about her the most. She nurtured and protected me the best way she knew. I remember at age 6, my mom would have random people come to our tiny one-bedroom apartment to get high with her. She would sit me in front of our living room television and place a piece of paper on our coffee table for me to draw on and say "Hey, don't you come in this kitchen!" Not even an hour later, the guy she let in grabbed my hand and tried to snatch me out of our front door. My mom quickly went into mama bear mode, grabbed my other hand, and pulled me back into the apartment just in time. She hurried and locked the screen door and held on to me tightly into her arms. While listening to her heart pound I heard her whisper in my ear, "I love you and I would never let anyone hurt you." From then on, she never let me out of her sight, and believe me, I'd never wanted to leave her side. Even though I was terrified, being in her arms felt like the safest place in the world. She also taught me this saying that she and I only know, and it goes...

Her: NEVER, NEVER, NEVER,

Me: LEAVE ME,

Her: I LOVE YOU MORE THAN THE WHOLE WIDE,

Me: WORLD,

Her: YOUR'E MY PRIDE AND,

Me: JOY.

From that moment on I looked at the world differently. The world was no longer a safe and happy place for me. I was always fearful and filled with anxiety whenever I had to leave my mom's side. I thought about how I could have been a victim of human trafficking, held captive in someone's creepy old dark basement, or even killed. Yes, I was put into horrifying situations, but now looking back as a parent, I do understand that there's no roadmap to parenting and my mom did the best she could under her circumstances. Regardless of what anyone says, nothing can take away the unconditional love I have for my mom.

Chapter 2

Childhood

At age 8, my dad found out my attendance at school was extremely poor. My mom's priorities were all messed up. She was always overprotective and too fearful of letting me out of her sight, so she would instead take me with her to random houses where she would get high. My dad decided to intervene and moved me in with him. I was devastated because my mom was my comfort zone. Even though my dad came around periodically, my mom was all I knew. What kid really wants to leave their mom? I know I didn't! We didn't care that our situation was dysfunctional and unfit, my mom and I had a bond that was unbreakable. I would have lived under a bridge with her if I had to. She was my rock, and I didn't want to let her go, but even at that young age, I knew it was time for me to release her and accept this situation. Honestly, I had no choice, and besides, I got tired of walking by schools and seeing little kids having fun, playing with their friends on the playground. I wanted to make friends and have fun too.

My mom ended up moving in with her new boyfriend and his daughter while I stayed with my dad, his girlfriend, her son and my older brother. I didn't get to see my mom on a daily basis like I used to, so my parents made an agreement for me to visit her on the weekends. I remember being so excited on Fridays after school because I knew she was going to take me somewhere. It never really felt like I was missing out on her being in my life because she would make sure we created memories with the trips she had planned. We would either go to the beach, watch my stepdad play drums at Will Rogers Park, or visit my cousins. Yeah… it was the simple things that brought excitement to my life back then. Each year she would always throw me these huge birthday parties too. I will never forget watching her do the Cha-Cha dance and singing oldie but goodies with friends, while my cousins and I wrestle in the jumper. She was always the life of the party and watching her as a social butterfly has always inspired me to be like her in some way.

Living with my dad was totally different from living with my mom. Living with him and being in school every day gave me a structured routine and brought a sense of stability into my life. I'd like to believe he is where I get my caring nature, sense of humor, and work ethic from. I watched my father go to work every day regardless of his achy feet and back pains. As a matter of fact, I've never really heard him complain about too much of anything. He'd always expressed how grateful he was just to be healthy enough to take care of his family with an honest job. He was also the type of man that care for other people children and not just his own. My dad made it his duty to take in family when they fell on hard times because it would kill him to see anyone living on the streets. Nowadays you don't get too many men like that. Watching how hard my dad worked to provide us with the best he could made me truly appreciate and respect him like no other. I wouldn't care if he decided to rob a bank today, he could do no wrong in my eyes.

He always told me, if you want to afford the nice things in life you would have to go out and work for it. Fast money ain't good money and nothing comes for free. Those words motivated me to work after school and during the summer throughout my high school years. Working as a teenager made me self-assured, taught me responsibility, and most importantly, forced me to appreciate the money I worked for. I worked as a youth educator for an after-school program called LA's best in Watts. My experience with inner city kids taught me what true patience was and it inspired me to want to be that young positive role model I wish I had growing up. Holding myself responsible to be the person that kids can talk to without them feeling like an outcast was important for me. This after school program also gave me the opportunity to sharpen my dance skills by putting me in a position to assist kids with their dance routines on their hip hop dance team.

My love for dance and music heightened around this time because clown dancing became very popular. Clown dancing is an urban style dance called krumping/clowning invented by Thomas Johnson aka Tommy the clown. He encouraged inner-city kids to join dance groups instead of gangs and I know from my own personal experience that clown dancing saved a lot of us from being bored and causing self-destruction. My friends and I were too occupied with constant practice of new dance routines and couldn't wait to show off our skills at the next house party. Man, it took me some time to learn the Heel Toe, Twerk and Krump, but I finally got the hang of it. The parties really didn't get started until the dance battles broke out. That's when you would take your best moves and individually freestyle against someone. In a way, dance battles gave us a different way to release all of our built up emotional and physical frustrations without unnecessary fighting or other self-sabotaging actions that could've potentially gotten us in trouble.

As I look back, we didn't have to smoke, drink, or pop pills, to have a good time at a party. It was like dancing stimulated us to have that feel good feeling to let loose, laugh, and enjoy each other's company. We looked forward to coming together, uplifting each other, and building stronger bonds through dancing as a group.

Another thing I noticed was how different genres of music positively and negatively impacted our lives by the way it influenced our thoughts and behaviors. In the 2000s, Young Jeezy music was all I heard around my neighborhood. It seemed like every guy I knew wanted to be dope boys and rob Nextel stores just to get rich quick, all because they were inspired to feel connected to the appearance and lifestyle of the Snowman. Unfortunately, a lot of my friends and family are in jail to this day because something as simple as music helped influence them to choose the wrong path. Growing up, a lot of us felt misunderstood and didn't have positive influences that we could look up to so connecting to music from people we related to made us feel a sense of belonging. Music is just that powerful, that it can boost your mood to make you happy or sad, redirect your focus from having road rage while sitting in a traffic jam, make you feel relaxed enough to fall asleep, and it can give you a positive or negative perspective on life.

Chapter 3

Independence

After I graduated high school, my dad decided to move from our home in Watts. I honestly believe that was the best decision he could've ever made because it forced everybody that was leaching off him to grow up and find their own way. Having previous work experience under my belt made me confident to lean on my independent decision-making skills to go out and find my footing in the world.

I decided to enroll in cosmetology school and work at FedEx part time. After I finished cosmetology school, I obtained my license, and found a hair salon to work in during the day while I continued to work at FedEx at night.

I eventually got my first apartment and fell in what I thought was love with my boyfriend from FedEx. I thought it was a good decision to move him in with me, and boy was I sadly mistaken. My boyfriend drank alcohol and smoked weed but so did every guy my age. Our relationship started off very loving and fast pace but then came the subtle verbal attacks. His indulgence in alcohol and weed got worse over time and so did our relationship. Eventually, he lost his job and started physically abusing me whenever he felt like everything in his world was spiraling out of control.

As I connect the dots today, I honestly believe I normalized abuse because I was surrounded by it in my household and in my community. Without sounding like I'm blaming myself, I do realize that violence, drinking, and drugs was something I was already familiar with, so the abuse didn't seem like much of a big problem in the beginning. I thought he was deeply in love with me when he started acting overprotective and controlling, not realizing how toxic, unhealthy, and codependent it was in reality.

After years of abuse, I finally stopped feeling ashamed and built up enough courage to ask my male cousin to help me get out of this chaotic situation. I asked my cousin to meet me at my apartment one night because I knew my boyfriend would be there waiting for me drunk as a skunk and high as a kite. As I walked in my apartment with my cousin following right behind me, my boyfriend's mouth dropped to the floor because he didn't expect me to walk in with a guy that was double his size in height and weight. My cousin kindly asked him to leave and not to come back. My boyfriend knew my cousin had just got out of jail, so it was easy for him to respect his wishes.

I thank God that I was able to get out of that situation with the help of my cousin because the relationship was going downhill fast. I'm grateful that neither one of us ended up in the hospital, behind bars, or buried six feet under. Being released from this abusive relationship made me rededicate my life to God, I started reattending my family's church called New Mount Calvary on Avalon and El Segundo. During my childhood my mom would force me to attend occasionally, but the purpose feels more meaningful when you want to voluntarily go on your own as an adult. Unfortunately, it takes a traumatic event to happen in our lives for us to turn back to God, but the church was the only place where I knew I could get the right guidance, encouragement, and strength for this next phase of my life.

Chapter 4

My mother's keeper

One night at work, I received a call from a family member telling me my mom was in the hospital. As my heart sank to my stomach, I immediately stopped everything I was doing to get there. When I got to the hospital, I saw my family with these sorrowful looks on their faces. I just knew something wasn't right and I'd immediately burst into tears. My uncle told me my mom had a brain aneurysm and Martin Luther King hospital didn't have the resources to properly treat her, and that they had to transport her to Harbor General hospital in Torrance. All types of thoughts were racing through my mind like, what if she doesn't make it? What would I do without her? What was our last conversation like? I know I wasn't ready to let my mom go so I went to God and prayed that if he helped her make it through this, I promise to take care of her. Well God did just that, her surgery was successful, and it took no time for my mom to learn how to walk and talk all over again. Even though her memory wasn't the same and she permanently had to walk with a cane, seems like throughout the past twelve years, nothing could really hold her back from getting more drugs and alcohol. Until this one incident…

One morning I decided to go check on my mom before my gym session. I noticed her door was wide open and the shoes she usually wear were sitting next to her sofa. Mind you, this was at two in the morning. I immediately ran in and yelled her name. I panicked as I heard no response from her, so I dialed 911. As I gave the dispatcher a description of her, I hoped and prayed to God, they could potentially help me find her. I was so relieved when the cop's truck finally pulled up to my mom's apartment. When I saw her step out the backseat of the police truck, I'd noticed she was barefoot with a bathmat in her hand. I asked her where she went and where did she get the bathmat from at two in the morning? She replied, "My police friend gave it to me." The officer and I glanced at each other, and he gave me a smirk, shaking his head saying, "No I didn't." I'd noticed my mom had dirt and leaves all down her back and I asked her if she fell. She told me yes and that she left her apartment because she locked herself out and couldn't find her keys. While conversing with her, I'd noticed her keys were on her lanyard, hanging around her neck the whole time.

I knew something wasn't right when she kept calling me her deceased sister's name, so I decided to stay with her at her apartment.

Usually, my mom will be able to do the majority of everything for herself with the slightest help from others, but this day was different. I'd usually get a call from her every day but now she couldn't remember how to use the phone. She almost set the kitchen on fire warming up food covered with foil in the microwave and mistakenly melting plastic in the oven. As I observed her bathing, I saw how she would confuse her kitchen oven mitts with bath washcloths, and I noticed she didn't even seem to realize she put her clothes on inside out and backwards at the same time. I've always helped take care of my mom throughout my adult life but this time I knew she had to live with me permanently. She already had memory loss from the brain aneurysm, but I knew this fall triggered something worse, so I took her to the doctor the next day. Her doctor evaluated her then diagnosed her with dementia. He said she needed to be cared for while under constant supervision. So, I took it into my hands to move her in with me. I couldn't help but to think back about the time I prayed to God, that if he pulled her through her surgery, I'd promised to take care of her. He did his part so now it was time for me to stand on my word and do mines.

People really underestimate the patience, strength, and understanding it takes to care for a parent twenty-four seven, especially when they speak and behave in inappropriate ways. It can be overwhelming with constant worry and stress, not only when you're trying to care for yourself, but for your husband and your kids too. I consistently dealt with guilt for taking on the role as a caregiver, being uncertain of how it would affect my marriage and family. Having my husband's approval and assistance really put everything at ease for me. He said there was no other solution, and that if it was his mom, he knew I would do the same for him. My husband's heart was as big as mine and it was situations like this that showed me why I agreed to marry him.

Chapter 5

Love at first sight

Let's rewind a little bit so I can tell you how I met my amazing husband. During my 20s I went through my clubbing phase. My home girls and I would go to clubs all throughout LA county. Our favorite spot was called The Bounce in Long beach. This club was a welcoming space not only for everybody but especially for plus size women to dress sexy and feel comfortable in their own skin while not feeling discriminated against.

One night, one of my homegirls got so drunk, she slapped the security guard and got us put out of the club. Why did she do that? IDK…We all know that one friend who gets aggressive when they have one too many drinks… While we were exiting the club, a group of Compton College football players were in line waiting to enter the club. As I walked by them, a guy grabbed my hand and looked me in the eyes and said, "Hey Sandra, you're so fine, can I get your number?" I looked up at him and asked him "How do you know my name?" he replied, "I heard your friend shouting it out loud rushing you to come out." We both chuckled and exchanged numbers. There was something different about this guy I met, not only was his name Dartonyon, so different from the typical names I'd usually hear, but his demeanor was so charismatic. Usually, guys wouldn't approach me the way that he did. I was impressed with how bold he was to step up to me, he grabbed my hand and looked me in my eyes, it actually caught me off guard at the same time.

Dartonyon and I talked over the phone every day since that night. He invited me to a function his football team were throwing on a Saturday night, and this was the night I knew I wanted him to be my husband. I brought my home girl with me to the function so I wouldn't feel alone just in case things didn't flow right at the party.

Dartonyon aka DJ greeted us at the door, he served us drinks, and introduced us to some of his teammates. I will never forget how lit the football team got when they heard the song Crank That by Soulja Boy. Seeing the strong bond, they shared off the football field while dancing together was really admiring. DJ and I danced to a couple of songs and then left the party. He walked my friend and I to the back house where he and another teammate lived. He told us to chill in there while he went to get more drinks for us.

As soon as he stepped out and closed the door behind him, my homegirl started scrambling and searching through his personal belongings.

You know how some girls like to go through guys' things just to see what they can find? Well, that was my homegirl. I was the total opposite. I was always too scared to find something that I didn't want to see. I barely knew this guy! My homegirl search was unsuccessful until she fumbled across an award from Bethany Prayer Temple church with DJ's name on it. It was an award for praying and my home girl saw that as a red flag. She got so accustomed to dating bad boys that good guys never really had a chance in her world. She said "Girl, if I were you, I wouldn't talk to him, he is a square! Oh no, we don't do squares!" We started laughing, but deep down inside my mind I was thinking

"THANK YOU JESUS!" I found me one! Now I knew I was dating a young, smart, athletic, handsome, God-fearing man that loves to party like I do. Yall know it's hard to find all those qualities in one man. That night I knew I could let my guard down just a little bit more. Two years later we got pregnant and 2 years after that we got married. Yes, in that order! We tried to do it the right way, but you know how life can get. Who's perfect?

Three months after my son was born, we got some terrifying news. We heard my stepbrother got murdered defending his girlfriend in a street fight. My stepbrother beat up the dude that was disrespecting his girlfriend, the dude got mad, took off to retrieve his gun, came back and killed my stepbrother. Not only was this news alarming but this tragedy happened right on the streets we grew up on in Watts. My family was devastated, but we knew it was time to move away from South Central Los Angeles. My husband and I couldn't take it anymore! It felt like everything was getting worse. The violence, the constant police harassment, and the sky-high rent was just enough for us to make a decision on leaving for good.

We refuse to raise our son in a place where we knew he couldn't be safe, even if we let him play in our front yard. The thought of us disconnecting from everything and everyone we knew was frightening, but we knew it had to happen for the betterment of not only our son's future but ours as well. So, we prayed on it and took a leap of faith.

Chapter 6

Taking a leap of Faith

My husband and I decided to relocate to the high desert. The cost of living was cheaper than LA, a little less populated, and we wouldn't be too far from our family. My husband worked graveyard shift at a warehouse while I worked during the day driving the city bus. We got pregnant and had another boy five years later.

After some time of working at the warehouse in Ontario, Ca, DJ was informed about his company opening a new warehouse in Reno NV. He came home excitedly telling me how he wanted to put his name on their relocation list, so he could have an opportunity to start fresh at a new location and potentially move up to a managerial position. He always felt like the supervisors at his current warehouse treated him unfairly and were always on his back about any and every little thing. He knew his current boss would never give him the chance to advance his skills to elevate at the warehouse he was at. He truly felt in his heart that relocating would give him another chance at connecting with new people to possibly get promoted so he could make more money to provide a better life for his family.

I agreed to the new start because it was important for me to support him in any way I could, and I didn't mind the change of scenery. I would go anywhere in the world with this man because he was home to me. So, we prayed on it and decided to pack up and move to Reno.

During our seven-hour drive to Reno, we were mesmerized by how beautiful the scenery was. Passing all the different types of tall beautiful trees, farms, and being up close to the snowy mountains really opened our eyes to all the nature we were missing out on by staying stuck in one state. Everything seemed so brand new compared to the old things we were used to seeing. This road trip made us forget about the past and motivated us to look forward to our future. It was astonishing to see how the city was building so many new housing communities and industrial warehouses all at once. You could tell the biggest little city was about to flourish into something bigger. It was something we totally wanted to be a part of.

Chapter 7

Heading into the unknown

As we prepared to settle into our new apartment and start this new beginning, everything started coming together. DJ liked his new job, the kids made new friends at their new school, and I started to get serious about my weight loss journey. During this time, Coronavirus was running rampant throughout the world and millions of people died in a short amount of time. We'd already survived the craziness of panic buying, and the quarantine phase of this pandemic but now covid vaccines were required to travel. Social distance, masking, and hand washing wasn't good enough any longer. We knew if we wanted to travel to see our family, we would have to get vaccinated. Even though we felt healthy and COVID free, we always had this constant worry about being a- symptomatic and passing COVID to our parents or grandparents. I mean we've all seen the effect it had on seniors with compromised immune systems. Like a lot of black and brown communities, our family suffered from chronic health conditions like diabetes, heart disease and lung disease, and it didn't help that they worked in essential fields like the healthcare and prisons systems.

At first, we were leery and indecisive about getting the COVID vaccination because there was just so much unknown about this whole COVID situation. Like where it actually came from, who it was affecting, to how fast they produced this vaccine, but with all the pressure from the news and family, constantly suggesting us to get vaccinated, we've decided to go for it. I remember my husband telling me to let him get the vaccine first to see what reaction he would get from it. Even though I admired how much of a protector he was, I refused to let him do that so I told him we were getting vaccinated together or there would be no getting vaccinated. So off we went to Walmart to get our first vaccine from Pfizer, scared of the unknown but proud of taking the first step to doing what's right. So, we thought....

We left Walmart with no reactions from the vaccine but the typical sore arm you usually get from getting any vaccine. After some days we came down with what felt like to be the common cold. You know how they tell you after getting the vaccine, you'll feel sick because that's your body's way of fighting off the infection from the vaccine. Well, we thought it was just that. We stayed in and rested some days but eventually, we went on with our daily tasks. Even though we moved into an apartment our goal was to buy a newly built construction home, so we drove around town to go look at what the city had to offer. Looking at new homes always made us excited and hopeful for our future, so doing that took our minds off things and made us feel a little better.

Not even two weeks after getting this vaccine my husband's health took a turn for the worst. He woke up one morning, turned to me, then said, "Oh shit, I can't move my legs, carry me to the restroom!" I rushed over to his side of our bed and put his arm around my neck so he could use my body as a crutch while he slowly dragged his feet to our bathroom. As I sat him on the toilet, I'd noticed he was having shortness of breath while he was saying "I'm trying but I cannot urinate." While we waited for the paramedics, I gave him a shower, as I sat him on the shower bench, he then shook his head and said ferociously "I regret getting this stupid ass shot! I felt good before getting it and now I feel like shit! Nothing could stop the tears from streaming down my face as I got him dressed. Uncertain of what was going to happen next left me feeling hopeless. My husband looked at me and asked me why I was crying. He tried to reassure me that everything was going to be alright and that he was strong enough to get through this. When the paramedics finally arrived, they asked me to help them carry my husband to the stretcher because he was too heavy for them. He was a little over six feet tall and weighed over three hundred pounds, but I was determined to get him to that stretcher even if I had to carry him all by myself. As we all counted to three and lifted him, I encouraged and reminded him that he was strong and to push himself to this stretcher that was just feet away. He eventually made it to the stretcher and as he laid back, he told me he loved me. I gave him a kiss and told him I loved him too and that I would see him at the hospital. My husband went into the hospital on a Sunday and died the next day on Monday.

    I had a very difficult time writing this chapter of the book because it brought up a lot of memories that I was trying to bury. Reliving those last days in my mind and thinking of the last words he said to me just shreds my heart to pieces. Because this traumatic event was so sudden and unexpected, it's hard for me to cope at times and it feels fresh like it happened yesterday. A lot of the time, I find myself trying to look at the lighter side of things by saying to myself, well, a lot of people didn't get to say I love you to their loved ones before they died, at least I did. I'm still in the process of learning that grief comes in waves, and it's okay for me to feel my emotions when I'm reminded of certain memories that were shared between us. I have to consistently remind myself that standing up to these painful feelings and accepting the reality of the situation is what's in fact helping me to heal.

Chapter 8

The Aftermath

No words can describe the heart wrenching pain I felt hearing that my husband was no longer here with us. I still can't believe it till this day. The hardest part was trying to hold my oldest son together while he fell apart as I told him his father died. He was in such disbelief because of how fast everything had happened. He said how could he have died so fast when he was just here with us yesterday? We were all so confused, and any answer that we did get for our questions, was never enough. This tragedy felt like a nightmare I couldn't wake up from. My whole life came to a screeching halt. What was I supposed to do now? Who was going to help me parent our two young black boys? Who was going to laugh at my unfunny jokes? I remember being so angry, angry with the whole world, angry with myself. I know we were taught not to question God, but for a split second, I was angry with Him too, I wanted answers! This was my best friend of 12 years, so who was I supposed to live this thing called life with now? I had so many questions and didn't want to hear anyone's answers. I didn't want to hear someone saying, "I'm sorry for your loss, or anyone telling me grieving will get easier with time. Deep down inside I was filled with resentment. All I could think of is why me? Why my family? I know that sounds harsh, but your perception becomes different when death comes knocking at your front door.

Even though I had a lot of family and friends around supporting me, I still felt like no one understood the position I was in. Everyone's suggestions on how I should grieve didn't take away the traumatizing pain or the unpredictable emotional roller coaster I was on every day. One minute I was fine and the next minute I would have these uncontrolled crying outbursts in the middle of the grocery store. I couldn't enjoy watching my favorite television shows because that was something we used to enjoy together, and it didn't feel right doing it without him. It felt impossible to complete my important daily tasks like I used to, I would even forget things like my keys and where I would park my car, and occasionally I would mentally check out during conversations due to loss of focus and lack of concentration. I felt like I was losing my mind and adapting to my reality while grieving was difficult to say the least.

I decided to seek help and confide in a therapist, she reassured me that my experiences were normal and that these were all temporary symptoms of widow's brain. I started to feel lonely and judged because people were comparing the way I grieve with the way they were grieving. You wouldn't believe some of the hurtful and inappropriate comments that were said to me at this time of mourning, I was told, stop all that crying, it's been long enough it's time to move on, it could have been worse, and do you think you need to be on medication? I'm not being insensitive to people that do have to take medication for grief symptoms, I just felt like people didn't care who or what I had just lost or even considered if I wanted to unalive myself by trying to dig me a deeper hole that I was already in. Man talk about kicking a person when they're down...

It was important for me to remove myself from certain people during this time because I was so irritable and emotional. I was like a ticking time bomb ready to explode at any given second. Even though some people probably meant well, I felt some people were choosing to be ignorant and their comments we're just needed to be left unsaid. I'd usually laugh things off but just because I was smiling on the outside didn't mean I wasn't hurting on the inside. I knew in order to keep my sanity, I had to distance myself from certain people that would trigger me. I even started to feel judged about looking too sad or too happy. Like my facial expressions determined if I was grieving correctly. I had to stop caring how people viewed the way I grieved because there is no right or wrong way to grieve, and when I decided to take a step back and quiet the noise surrounding me, I realized that time to myself gave me clarity on what I was feeling on the inside. My newly found peace gave me the ability to think more clearly and freely despite the chaos around me.

My boys dealt with countless anxiety-filled meltdowns and panic attacks during this time. They would cling on to me so tight because they were so afraid something would happen to me next. They had lost their dad and couldn't stand the thought of losing their mom. What made matters worse was when cruel kids from their school bullied them about their dad dying. There were times when my 11-year-old son would cry to me, blaming himself for the death of his dad. My husband was very close to our boys and played a very significant role in their lives, so I knew this grieving process would be difficult for them too. I would break down in tears, give him a big hug, and reassure him that he didn't have to be strong all the time and it was absolutely normal to release those emotions by crying, talking, writing, playing or whatever expression that made them feel comfortable. Millions of people have died during this covid pandemic, and it wasn't anyone's fault. I had to be up front with my boys and tell them that death is a normal part of life and we're all here on this earth temporarily.

The constant stress, headaches, anxiety, depression, body aches, confusion, and exhaustion were killing me. The lack of concentration, appetite, and sleep were interfering with my day-to-day life. Most days I just wanted to lay in bed and cry but staying in that phase would have been unfair to my kids and mom because I knew they were depending on me, and I was the only one responsible for them now. My boys were my motivation to pull myself together and I needed to lead them by example. I had to humble myself and ask God for forgiveness, I needed Him to forgive me for losing faith and trust in Him at this time of confusion and pain. I asked Him for strength, understanding, and guidance during this time of mourning. I had to remind myself that even though I felt alone, God was right there by my side especially in this time of despair. It was important for me to stop focusing on what I no longer had and learn to be thankful and show gratitude for everything I did have.

I needed to provide a sense of normalcy to our lives, so we moved back to our home in the high desert. When I pulled up to our home, I broke down in tears. Thinking about all the old memories we shared in our first home. Walking through those doors reminded me of when we finally closed on our home and received our keys, my husband wanted to pick me up and carry me through the doors like they do in the movies, but when he tried, he struggled and dropped me before we could even get through the door, or the time he almost put our house on fire trying to display fireworks for our kids on the 4th of July.

Next, I enrolled my boys in school, and registered them in sport activities, like track and field and football to keep all of us busy. This was their first time in track and field, and they surprisingly excelled at it. They made the All-Star team, so we got the opportunity to travel and compete in different states. Engaging in programs like this definitely boosted my boys' confidence and introduced them to a group of new friends with the same interest. Most importantly, it positively redirected their attention to something they loved to do. Right before my husband died, we talked about living our best lives and traveling more. So, when the boys weren't at school, track meets, games, personal training, or practice. I would plan trips for us to enjoy the little free time we did have together. We would enjoy our time at different theme parks, cruises, and various vacation spots where we could kick back, relax and enjoy activities we normally wouldn't get involved in.

Even though God has blessed us with a great life, I wanted to show my boys that it was important to be a blessing to people who weren't as fortunate by being kind, generous and by giving back. Some of these acts of kindness would be donating clothes to our local women's shelter, surprising the person in line behind us by paying for their items and cooking up big Thanksgiving meals to pass out to the homeless. It really fills my heart to give, so hopefully I will pass on my big-hearted trait by showing my boys when you do things with a pure heart, good intentions, and with no expectations, God will continue to bless you in many ways that man can't. Seeing other dads cheering their kids on at games or even playing in the pool on family vacations made our hearts yearn for the love we shared as a family, but I try to remind myself that I know my husband is smiling down on us and he's proud of the life I'm providing for our two smart, strong, caring, handsome young men that we've created.

Chapter 9

Self-Care

All the extracurricular activities we were involved in kept us so busy that time flew past us. Not only was it time to remember the most tragic day of the year but this day fell in the fall season. Everything felt dark because the days got gloomier, and the holidays were approaching. Getting through the first year seemed easier than getting through the second year. Seemed like all my family and friends went back to living their lives like normal and I was stuck in the same cycle of a nightmare. Since all the activities were over, I had time to actually sit with my feelings and not suppress those painful emotions I've been trying to avoid. I had to start accepting my uncomfortable reality and it was time to move forward.

Like the majority of moms, I would be too busy taking care of everybody else first and putting my-self-care and the things that I enjoy last. Not only was grieving extremely difficult, but I had myself, my boys, and my mom to look after. I knew if I wanted to shift my mood and get myself out of this depressing wave of emotions, I had to intentionally carve out time to do things for myself.

I thought back to the activities that I used to do that were fulfilling and remembered how excited home decorating made me feel, so I started small remodeling projects around the house that would give my home a fresh new feel. I started indulging in self-care services by going to the spa for relaxing massages, manicures, and pedicures which helped relief stress and reduce built up tension. Retail therapy was one of my all-time favorites and has always made me feel better, but I knew if I wasn't careful with that one it could quickly turn into an addiction. I found that the most cost efficient and biggest mood booster of all time was listening and dancing to music. This was something I loved but stopped doing because I went through a phase when I couldn't listen to gospel music because I would immediately breakdown into tears. I couldn't tolerate listening to love songs either because it reminded me of the love I no longer had, so I turned to upbeat music that uplifted me and made me want to get up and dance.

I constantly played upbeat music in the background because I couldn't stand to sit in silence with my thoughts. My mind was overwhelmingly consumed with thoughts of sadness, loneliness, and other feelings, so I would play music while I cooked and cleaned, but I really fell in love with shower singing and car karaoke. Music helped me balance my emotions especially when I incorporated dance with it.

One day I was scrolling on YouTube, looking up popular dance fitness videos and this one video caught my eye. What captured my interest was this group of black women dancing to hip hop music. This dance fitness class that promoted self-love and body positivity was called Trap Cardio. It was refreshing to see everyday women that I could relate to, using their natural bodies to attain their desired weight loss results. I felt no pressure about where I was mentally or physically on my weight loss journey because everyone in the class was all different shapes and ages. I know it sounds unorthodox, but it can be unrealistic and discouraging to stay motivated by people who have the perfect body that would never look like mines. Some days I would catch myself dancing for three hours because it felt good to redirect my focus on something else other than the loss of my husband. Adding Trap Cardio to my workout routine was super convenient because I could workout at home anytime of the day and still be attentive to my mom's needs. Trap cardio reminded me of how I used to use music and dance, to express all the different emotions and feelings that were bottled up inside of me. It distracted me from the pain I felt inside and helped me to creatively express that pain on the outside. As I found myself 50 pounds lighter, I've noticed how vital it was for my healing process to indulge in activities that I've once loved to do. My self-confidence boosted, I was much more excited about life, and I was able to sleep through the night because I wasn't as stressed. Everything in my life automatically felt a little bit lighter as I got lighter.

Chapter 10

Listening to my intuition

One morning after dropping my boys off at school I'd noticed there was shattered glass on the front side of our house. I remembered the shattered glass came from the window my husband broke. He broke our house window because he had to show his supervisor proof that somebody had tried to break into our house. Yeah, it was a lie, but it was a desperate attempt to get a valid excuse to miss work. We needed to sign some important paperwork in Reno and if he missed any days of work, they would've taken him off the relocation list. Seeing that shattered glass lying right up against our home made me sit down and think of all the other obstacles that were trying to stop us from moving to Reno.

Like when his supervisor took him off the relocation list because of some minor incident that happened at work or when we had our cars all packed up the day of the move and one of our cars wouldn't start. We called AAA for a jump, AAA came and checked the battery, but had to leave because their battery charger wasn't strong enough to give our car a jump. The AAA technician was supposed to have come right back but never did. Not for one second did we stop and think that God was trying to give us a sign not to move to Reno, we just replaced the old battery with a brand-new battery. We took those red flags and said that the devil was working hard and trying to keep us from moving forward. We had already signed up for the relocation, so it wasn't like we could change our minds about the move anyways.

But now that I look back as a widow, I think what if that was God trying to give us warnings, signaling us to stay?

Reflecting on the death of my husband and some of the traumatizing events that has occurred in my life has made me realize how resilient I truly am. These past events have forced me to search for meaning in my life and encouraged me to evolve as a person. I've always struggled with finding my purpose in life, but what I've learned is that serving a purpose is much more easier and being productive in the things that I'm passionate about has been like a personal guide to a much more fulfilling life. I now understand that when traumatizing events happen, that they are just life's tests and challenges that I need to face in order to propel me to become the person that I am meant to be, so just remember to never give up on yourself and know that God gives his toughest battles to his strongest soldiers.

BE YOUR OWN INSPIRATION

A lot of my life I'd felt misunderstood which led me to feel like I had no one to turn to. I turned to paper to write down and express my inner thoughts and emotions that I'd suppressed for a very long time. Writing has really helped my healing journey and relieved some of the pain that I didn't realize I was still holding on to. I'm in high hopes that this book will encourage you to start your healing process through writing as I have. Remember that nobody can tell your story, your feelings are valid, and it's not about where you start, but how you finish!

Journal With Me

I hope you enjoyed my book thank you for growing with me throughout my book journey may blessings continue to flourish in your life.

- Sandra Loyd

www.ingramcontent.com/pod-product-compliance
Lightning Source LLC
Chambersburg PA
CBHW071225160426
43196CB00012B/2414